JOSEPH
and his BROTHERS

illustrated by Leon Baxter

adapted by Philip Steele

Macdonald

There was once a Pharaoh of Egypt who liked to ride in his chariot along the banks of the River Nile. Every morning he would look at the fields of golden corn and smile happily. A good harvest meant a full belly for everyone in his kingdom, and no trouble for the Pharaoh!

One day he returned to the palace to find Joseph, the Lord Governor of Egypt, waiting for him.

'Joseph! How nice to see you!' exclaimed the Pharaoh. 'Another bumper crop this year, eh? I trust our grain stores are all full?'

'Your Highness,' said Joseph, 'they are overflowing. For seven years now we have had good harvests. But do you remember the dreams you had, and what they meant? Seven years of plenty will be followed by seven years of famine. From now on we must live only on the grain we have stored.'

'Quite so,' said the Pharaoh gravely. 'Bother!' he added under his breath. Could this Joseph be trusted? After all, not so long ago he had been a mere prisoner in the city jail, a slave from Canaan or some such place. The Pharaoh's day was quite spoilt.

Joseph was not wrong. The following spring the seed was sown as usual. Green shoots appeared – but they soon turned brown and died. Anxious people came from all over Egypt, and gathered in crowds around the royal palace. Joseph came out to speak to them.

'There's nothing to worry about,' he told them. 'We now have enough grain stored away to last us seven years – and more besides.'

The Egyptians might have enough to eat, but nobody else did. In Canaan, and the other lands to the east, the crops failed and the rivers dried up. Joseph's father, Jacob, still lived in Canaan. Jacob prayed to God that he and his family would not die of hunger. Then, one day, a passing merchant brought the news that corn was on sale in Egypt. Jacob called his sons together.

'You must travel to Egypt and buy some corn with my savings,' he said. 'It's our only chance.'

'A journey to Egypt! How exciting!' exclaimed Benjamin, the youngest of Jacob's sons.

'You will not be going,' said Jacob sternly. 'Your brothers are old enough to look after themselves, but you are my dearest and youngest son, and you must stay here – just in case they run into trouble.'

The brothers set out on their donkeys, with Reuben and Simeon leading the way, and Judah at the back. It was a long journey, and they were soon hungry and thirsty.

'We are being punished by God,' said Judah.

'It's my fault,' said Simeon sadly. 'It was I who sold our brother Joseph as a slave.'

'And it was I who lied to father,' added Reuben. 'I told him that Joseph had been killed by a wild animal.'

After many days the brothers reached the capital city of Egypt. They gazed around them in amazement. There were huge temples and statues, and streets full of people. Then they asked where they could buy corn.

The brothers were directed to the royal granary. There they joined a long queue outside the office of the Lord Governor.

When the doors were opened the brothers saw a room full of clerks, money changers, and slaves carrying sacks of corn. Sitting on a throne was a tall man wearing the clothes of an Egyptian nobleman. They went up to him and bowed low. They didn't realize that this stranger was their long-lost brother. But Joseph recognized them, and smiled to himself. Why should he tell them who he was? They would find out soon enough.

Joseph put on his fiercest voice, and spoke to his brothers in the Egyptian language.

'On your feet!' he snapped. 'Who are you? Where do you come from?' He turned to a clerk. 'Here, these fools do not understand Egyptian. Translate what they have to say.'

Reuben stepped forward nervously.

'If it please your honour, we've come all the way from Canaan to buy corn.'

'Oho!' roared Joseph. 'And how do I know that you are not spies? I suppose you have sneaked in here to find out the Pharaoh's secrets?'

'N–No my lord!' stammered Levi. We are honest folk. Our father is Jacob, a good man.'

'And are you the only sons he has?' asked Joseph through the interpreter.

'Yes,' said Levi. 'Except for young Benjamin, who stayed at home. And Joseph, who er . . . had an unfortunate accident some years ago. We haven't seen him since.'

Joseph raised his eyebrows. 'I see!' Then he snapped his fingers for the guards. 'Lock up these men until I decide what to do with them!' he ordered.

The brothers looked so miserable, Joseph had to wipe a tear from his eye. But he was not yet ready to forgive them.

On their third day in Egypt, Joseph sent for his brothers again.

'You can go now,' he said. 'Here is all the corn you wanted. But you must still prove that you are telling the truth. You must return with Benjamin. Until I see him with my own eyes, one of you will be kept here as a hostage.' His gaze fell on Simeon, who was immediately led off by the guards.

The brothers were sad as they rode away. They had the corn, it was true, but they had left Simeon in jail in a foreign land.

That night the brothers pitched camp in a rocky valley. Judah went to check the baggage, and opened a sack of corn. Lying on top of the grain was a bag of money. He counted out the coins by the light of the fire – it was the money they had paid for the corn! The brothers were really scared now. Supposing the Governor had sent soldiers after them, to accuse them of theft? The brothers broke camp and hurried homewards.

When the brothers reached home, they found to their amazement that every sack of corn had a bag of money inside! Jacob was very worried when they told him what had happened.

'Who is this Lord Governor?' he questioned his sons. 'Why didn't he trust you? And why did you have to tell him about Benjamin?'

'The Governor is the most important man in Egypt after the Pharaoh,' explained Reuben. 'I don't know why he was so suspicious, but we could hardly argue with him. Benjamin must come back with us to Egypt.'

Jacob shook his head sadly and stared out at his empty fields. He had lost Joseph. Now he had lost Simeon. He couldn't bear to lose young Benjamin as well.

'Benjamin must stay here in Canaan,' he commanded.

Most of the corn they had bought was ground into flour, and during the winter months there was enough bread to feed everyone. Part of the corn was put to one side, and this was used to sow the fields in the spring. Once again green shoots appeared, but once again they died. Even Jacob agreed that there was no choice this time. The brothers would have to go back to Egypt – with Benjamin.

The brothers hardly spoke a word on the journey back to Egypt, they were so frightened. They took special gifts for the Lord Governor – myrrh, honey, spices and almonds. They took twice as much money as the corn would cost, and to be on the safe side they took back the money they had found in the sacks.

When they arrived in the city, they were surprised to be sent in to see the Lord Governor straight away. Joseph saw that young Benjamin was with his brothers. He was overjoyed, but decided to say nothing for the time being. He told his servant to make the travellers comfortable, and to set Simeon free. Reuben started to explain to the servants about the money they had found in the sacks, but Joseph had told the servants what to say.

'Don't worry,' they replied. 'We did take your money. It was your God who put the coins in your sacks.'

Two hours later, Simeon and the brothers were sitting down to a splendid feast. They were eating the same food as the Governor himself, and Benjamin's plate was piled higher than anyone else's. It was all most puzzling.

16

The brothers set out on the journey home at dawn. But before they left, Joseph had a word with his servant.

'Fill up their sacks with food and money,' he whispered. 'Then take my silver cup and hide it in the sack of the youngest one.'

The brothers had been travelling for less than an hour when they were overtaken by a speeding chariot. The driver reined in his pair of fine horses.

'Stop in the name of the Pharaoh!' shouted the driver. 'You are charged with the theft of a silver cup!'

The brothers protested noisily, but it was no use. The sacks were opened and there, amongst Benjamin's share of the grain, was a shining cup. They were taken back to the city, and brought before Joseph.

'Well, this is a fine way to repay my kindness!' he said to them. 'I shall have to take the thief as my slave.'

The brothers looked at Joseph in horror.

'Let me be your slave!' cried Judah. 'Our father is an old man. If we return without little Benjamin, it will break his heart. He has already lost one son.'

'Oh, take them away!' said Joseph to the guards. He sat all alone on his throne, and wept as though his heart would break. He had made his family suffer enough.

So Joseph called his brothers back into the room.

'I am your own brother,' he said, wiping away his tears, '. . . Joseph – whom you sold as a slave. It wasn't your fault. God planned it all, so that I could save your lives one day!'

The brothers were confused. How could this Egyptian nobleman be their own flesh and blood? Why was he speaking to them in their own language? Suddenly everyone was laughing and crying. The Pharaoh heard the merriment and came to see what was going on.

'Long lost family, eh? I say! Delighted to meet you all!' He shook them by the hand. 'Why don't you all come and live in Egypt?'

Joseph laughed. 'The Pharaoh is right. Take these gifts of clothes and food and silver, and return to Canaan. Tell Father to bring all our people and our flocks into Egypt. The famine will last another five years, but here there is enough food for everyone.'

And so it was that Jacob and his sons and their families came to move from Canaan down into Egypt. The old man wept with happiness when he saw Joseph again, and through all the years of hardship God looked after them in their new home.

This story has been told in many different ways for more than three thousand years. It was first written down in a language called Hebrew. Since then it has been re-told in almost every language used in the world today.

You can find the story of Joseph in the Bible. This part of his life is in the Book of Genesis, Chapters 41 to 46.

There is a companion to this book called 'Joseph and his Coat of Many Colours'. It tells how Joseph quarrelled with his brothers, and how they sold him into slavery in Egypt.